she
believed
she could
so
she did

DATE: 1 / 21 / 2024

Sam Davis— go over life insurance
(Split Chuck / Carah)

Questions for attorney:

Deed— Transfer upon Death?

DATE:___/___/___

think positive

"The best way to gain self-confidence is to do what you are afraid to do." – Unknown

"Have dreams and dream big!
Dream without fear"

MAKE IT HAPPEN

DATE:___/___/___

think positive

"Believe in miracles but above all believe in yourself!"

DATE:____/____/____

"Let your dreams be as big
as your desire to succeed"

BELIEVE
YOU CAN

DATE:___/___/___

think positive

"Never downgrade your dreams, reach for the stars and believe in your self power"

DATE:___/___/___

BELIEVE IN YOURSELF

DATE:___/___/___

think
positive

"Never be afraid to start something new,
if you fail it is just temporary, if you believe and
persist you will succeed"

DATE:___/___/___

DATE:___/___/___

think
positive

"Wherever you go, go with all your heart." - Confucius

DATE:____/____/____

DATE:___/___/___

think
positive

"Your dreams and your goals are the seeds
of your own success"

DATE:____/____/____

MAKE IT HAPPEN

DATE:___/___/___

think positive

"Start where you are and take chances"

DATE:____/____/____

BELIEVE YOU CAN

DATE:___/___/___

think positive

"Life isn't about finding yourself.
Life is about creating yourself." - George Bernard Shaw

DATE:___/___/___

"Keep your motivation and your momentum
with a new goal every day!"

BELIEVE IN YOURSELF

DATE: ___ / ___ / ___

think positive

"CHANGE YOUR LIFE TODAY. DON'T GAMBLE ON THE FUTURE, ACT NOW, WITHOUT DELAY." — SIMONE DE BEAUVOIR

DATE:___/___/___

"The person who says it cannot be done should not interrupt the person who is doing it." – Chinese Proverb

TAKE ACTION!

DATE:___/___/___

think positive

"AIM FOR THE STARS TO KEEP YOUR DREAMS ALIVE"

DATE:___/___/___

"There are no limits to what you can
Achieve if you believe in your dreams"

think
positive

"When you feel you are defeated, just remember,
you have the power to move on,
it is all in your mind"

DATE:___/___/___

"Don't just dream your dreams, make them happen!"

MAKE IT HAPPEN

DATE:___/___/___

think
positive

"OPPORTUNITY COMES TO THOSE WHO NEVER GIVE UP"

DATE:___/___/___

BELIEVE YOU CAN

DATE:___/___/___

think positive

"ALWAYS AIM FOR BIGGER GOALS, THEY HAVE
THE POWER TO KEEP YOU MOTIVATED"

DATE:___/___/___

BELIEVE IN YOURSELF

DATE:___/___/___

think
positive

"SUCCESS IS NOT A PLACE OR A DESTINATION,
IT IS A WAY OF THINKING WHILE ALWAYS
HAVING A NEW GOAL IN MIND"

DATE:___/___/___

"Fall seven times and stand up eight." –
Japanese Proverb

DATE:___/___/___

think
positive

"CHANGE THE WORLD ONE DREAM AT A TIME,
BELIEVE IN YOUR DREAMS"

DATE:___/___/___

never give up

DATE:___/___/___

think positive

"Never loose confidence in your dreams,
there will be obstacles and defeats, but you will
always win if you persist"

DATE:___/___/___

"Dreams are the energy that power your life"

DATE:___/___/___

think positive

"Never wait for someone else to validate your existence, you are the creator of your own destiny"

DATE:___/___/___

"Always dream big and follow your heart"

BELIEVE YOU CAN

think
positive

"Everything you dream is possible
as long as you believe in yourself"

DATE:___/___/___

BELIEVE IN YOURSELF

DATE:___/___/___

think positive

"A SUCCESSFUL PERSON IS SOMEONE THAT UNDERSTANDS
TEMPORARY DEFEAT AS A LEARNING PROCESS, NEVER GIVE UP!"

DATE:___/___/___

TAKE ACTION!

DATE:___/___/___

think positive

"MOTIVATION COMES FROM WORKING ON OUR DREAMS AND
FROM TAKING ACTION TO ACHIEVE OUR GOALS"

DATE:___/___/___

DATE:___/___/___

think positive

"Your mission in life should be to thrive
and not merely survive"

DATE:___/___/___

MAKE IT HAPPEN

DATE:___/___/___

think
positive

"DOING WHAT YOU BELIEVE IN, AND GOING AFTER YOUR
DREAMS WILL ONLY RESULT IN SUCCESS." - ANONYMOUS

DATE:___/___/___

"Be brave, fight for what you believe
in and make your dreams a reality."

BELIEVE
YOU CAN

DATE:___/___/___

think positive

"The will to win, the desire to succeed, the urge to reach your full potential... these are the keys that will unlock the door to personal excellence." – Confucius

DATE:___/___/___

BELIEVE IN
YOURSELF

DATE: ___/___/___

think positive

"LET YOUR DREAMS BE BIGGER THAN YOUR FEARS AND YOUR ACTIONS
LOUDER THAN YOUR WORDS." - ANONYMOUS

DATE:___/___/___

TAKE ACTION!

DATE:___/___/___

think
positive

"START EVERY DAY WITH A GOAL IN MIND AND
MAKE IT HAPPEN WITH YOUR ACTIONS"

DATE:___/___/___

never give up

think positive

"If you have big dreams you will always
have big reasons to wake up every day"

DATE:___/___/___

"To achieve our dreams we must first overcome our fear of failure"

think
positive

"Difficulties are nothing more than
opportunities in disguise, keep on
trying and you will succeed"

DATE:___/___/___

**BELIEVE
YOU CAN**

DATE:___/___/___

think positive

"Always have a powerful reason to wake up
every new morning, set goals and follow your dreams"

DATE:___/___/___

"Have faith in the future but above all in yourself"

BELIEVE IN YOURSELF

DATE:___/___/___

think positive

"NEVER LET YOUR DREAMS DIE FOR FEAR OF FAILURE.
DEFEAT IS JUST TEMPORARY: YOUR DREAMS ARE YOUR POWER"

DATE:___/___/___

TAKE ACTION!

DATE:___/___/___

think
positive

"A FAILURE IS A LESSON, NOT A LOSS. IT IS A TEMPORARY
AND SOMETIMES NECESSARY DETOUR, NOT A DEAD END"

DATE:___/___/___

"Your future is created by what you do today not tomorrow" - Anonymous

never give up

DATE: ___/___/___

think positive

DATE:___/___/___

"Don't go into something to test the waters, go into things to make waves"
— Anonymous

MAKE IT HAPPEN

DATE:___/___/___

think positive

"Laughter is the shock absorber that softens and minimizes the bumps of life" — Anonymous

DATE:___/___/___

"Dream – Believe – Achieve"

BELIEVE YOU CAN

DATE:___/___/___

think positive

"HOPE IS A WAKING DREAM" - ARISTOTLE

DATE:___/___/___

BELIEVE IN YOURSELF

DATE:___/___/___

think positive

"NEVER GIVE UP ON A DREAM JUST BECAUSE OF THE TIME IT WILL TAKE
TO ACCOMPLISH IT. THE TIME WILL PASS ANYWAY."
– ANONYMOUS

DATE:___/___/___

TAKE ACTION!

DATE:___/___/___

think positive

"IF YOU WANT TO FEEL RICH, JUST COUNT ALL THE THINGS
YOU HAVE THAT MONEY CAN'T BUY" — ANONYMOUS

DATE:____/____/____

"It does not matter how slowly you go as long as you do not stop" – Confucius

never give up

DATE:___/___/___

think
positive

"Some pursue success and
happiness – Others create it"
— Anonymous

DATE:___/___/___

MAKE IT HAPPEN

DATE:___/___/___

think
positive

"IT'S BETTER TO HAVE AN IMPOSSIBLE DREAM THAN
NO DREAM AT ALL" – ANONYMOUS

DATE:___/___/___

BELIEVE YOU CAN

DATE:___/___/___

think positive

"The winner always has a plan; The loser always has an excuse" — Anonymous

DATE:___/___/___

BELIEVE IN YOURSELF

DATE:___/___/___

"There is no elevator to success.
you have to take the stairs"
— Anonymous

DATE:___/___/___

TAKE ACTION!

"Never let defeat have the last word" — Anonymous

DATE:___/___/___

think positive

"DON'T LET YESTERDAY'S DISAPPOINTMENTS, OVERSHADOW
TOMORROW'S ACHIEVEMENTS" — ANONYMOUS

DATE:___/___/___

DATE:___/___/___

think
positive

"WE ARE LIMITED, NOT BY OUR ABILITIES, BUT BY OUR VISION"
— ANONYMOUS

DATE:___/___/___

MAKE IT HAPPEN

DATE:___/___/___

think positive

"A JOURNEY OF A THOUSAND MILES MUST BEGIN
WITH A SINGLE STEP." – LAO TZU

DATE:___/___/___

BELIEVE YOU CAN

DATE: ___/___/___

think
positive

"A diamond is a chunk of coal that
made good under pressure"
— Anonymous

DATE: ___/___/___

BELIEVE IN YOURSELF

_____
_____
_____
_____
_____
_____
_____
_____
_____
_____
_____
_____
_____
_____
_____
_____
_____
_____
_____
_____
_____
_____
_____
_____
_____
_____
_____
_____
_____

DATE:___/___/___

think positive

DATE:___/___/___

"Wherever you go, go with all your heart" – Confucius

DATE:___/___/___

"Dream is not what you see in sleep, dream is the thing
which does not let you sleep" — Anonymous

DATE:___/___/___

"All our tomorrows depend on today" — *Anonymous*

DATE:____/____/____

think positive

"DON'T BE PUSHED BY YOUR PROBLEMS.
BE LED BY YOUR DREAMS" — ANONYMOUS

DATE:___/___/___

MAKE IT HAPPEN

DATE: ___/___/___

think
positive

"ONCE YOU HAVE A DREAM PUT ALL YOUR HEART
AND SOUL TO ACHIEVE IT"

DATE:____/____/____

BELIEVE YOU CAN

DATE:___/___/___

think positive

"YOU CREATE YOUR LIFE BY FOLLOWING
YOUR DREAMS WITH DECISIVE ACTIONS"

DATE:___/___/___

"Without dreams you lose interest in life; you have no energy to move forward"

BELIEVE IN YOURSELF

DATE: ___/___/___

think positive

"The road to success is always full of surprises
and temporary failures, real success comes
to those who persist and enjoy the journey"

DATE:___/___/___

TAKE ACTION!

think positive

"TO live a creative life, we must lose
our fear of being wrong"
- Anonymous

DATE:___/___/___

never give up

DATE: ___/___/___

think positive

"MAKE EACH DAY COUNT, YOU WILL NEVER
HAVE THIS DAY AGAIN"

"It's not what you look at that matters,
it's what you see" - Anonymous

MAKE IT HAPPEN

DATE:___/___/___

think
positive

"SUCCESSFUL PEOPLE MAKE A HABIT OF DOING WHAT
UNSUCCESSFUL PEOPLE DON'T WANT TO DO"
— ANONYMOUS

DATE:___/___/___

BELIEVE
YOU CAN

"Nothing worth having comes easy"
- Anonymous

DATE:___/___/___

think positive

Be Strong! It might be stormy
now, but it can't rain forever!"
- Anonymous

DATE:___/___/___

BELIEVE IN YOURSELF

DATE:____/____/____

"Be Strong! It might be stormy now, but it can't rain forever!" - Anonymous
"

DATE:___/___/___

BELIEVE IN YOURSELF

DATE:___/___/___

BELIEVE IN YOURSELF

DATE:___/___/___

"It doesn't matter what you look like on the outside. It's what's on the inside that counts"
- Unknown

BELIEVE IN YOURSELF

DATE:___/___/___

BELIEVE IN YOURSELF

DATE:___/___/___

BELIEVE IN YOURSELF

DATE:___/___/___

BELIEVE IN YOURSELF

DATE:___/___/___

"Be Strong – Be Brave – Keep Going"

BELIEVE IN YOURSELF

DATE:___/___/___

"Don't let a bad day make you feel like you have a bad life" – Unknown

DATE:___/___/___

BELIEVE IN YOURSELF

CREATIVE JOURNALS
FACTORY

WE HOPE YOU LIKED YOUR JOURNAL - NOTEBOOK
PLEASE WRITE YOUR REVIEW, IT MEANS A LOT TO US!

DESIGNED BY:

CREATIVE JOURNALS FACTORY

THANK YOU!

Made in the USA
Las Vegas, NV
15 November 2023